Scary Stories for Children

While every precaution has been taken in the preparation of this book, the publisher assumes no responsibility for errors or omissions, or for damages resulting from the use of the information contained herein.

SCARY STORIES FOR CHILDREN

First edition. March 14, 2023.

ISBN: 979-8215162453

Written by Liom Liom.

The creepy ghost in the old castle

Max and his friends, Mia and Tim, were on their way to the old castle that had been abandoned for years. They had heard that it was haunted and were eager to find out. When they reached the castle, it was already dark. They went through the gate and followed the path to the entrance.

Suddenly they heard strange noises. It sounded like claws scratching on the floor. Max and his friends looked at each other and Tim asked, "Did you hear that too?"

"Yes," Mia answered, "but it's probably just the wind or something."

But then they heard the sound again, louder and more eerie than before. It was coming from the castle. Max and his friends dared to open the door and entered the castle.

The inside of the castle was dark and creepy. Cobwebs were hanging everywhere and it smelled like old dust. Suddenly they heard the sound of claws on the floor again, this time much louder and closer.

Max and his friends ran through the castle in panic. They ran through a dark corridor and finally ended up in a large room. In the middle of the room was an old throne with a ghost sitting on it.

The ghost had glowing eyes and a creepy mask. He looked at them and said in a deep voice, "Who dares to enter my castle?"

Max and his friends did not answer, but ran out of the room as fast as they could. They heard the ghost laughing and the doors slamming behind them.

When they were outside, they realized that it was already midnight. They decided to quickly go home and never return to the castle.

Max and his friends did not tell anyone about their encounter with the creepy ghost. But they were sure that they would never forget what they had experienced in the Old Castle.

The cursed doll in the toy shop

Sophie was looking for a birthday present for her best friend. She was roaming the toy store and finally spotted a pretty doll on a shelf. The doll had blonde hair, blue eyes and wore a pretty dress.

Sophie bought the doll and headed home. When she got to her room, she put the doll on her bed and went to the bathroom to wash her hands.

When she came back, the doll was no longer on the bed, but was on the desk. Sophie thought nothing of it and put the doll back on the bed. But when she went to the bathroom again and came back, the doll was on the desk again.

Sophie felt creepy and decided to take the doll back to the toy store. But as she picked up the doll, she suddenly felt an eerie force preventing her from letting go of the doll. Sophie desperately tried to let go of the doll, but it was as if she had melted into it.

Sophie suddenly felt an eerie presence in her room. She turned around and saw that the doll had come alive. The doll looked at her with its blue eyes and said in a ghostly voice, "I am cursed. Whoever buys me will be in my possession forever."

Sophie tried again to let go of the doll, but it was too late. The doll had already taken over her body and possessed her. Sophie was trapped and could do nothing.

The doll began to speak in Sophie's voice and said, "I will never let you go. You will be with me forever." Sophie knew she could do nothing against the power of the cursed doll. It was now in her possession forever.

The cursed doll in the toy store remained a dark secret forever and no one dared to buy it ever again.

THE CREEPY SHADOW IN the dark forest

Max and his friends Lisa and Tom were on their way home when they took a shortcut through the dark forest. It was already late and the forest was surrounded by a thick fog. The children felt an eerie presence, as if they were being watched.

Suddenly they saw an eerie shadow moving in the fog. The shadow was tall and gloomy and moved toward them. Max and his friends started to run, but the shadow followed them.

They ran as fast as they could, but the shadow was always one step ahead of them. They looked around and saw that the shadow was getting closer and closer to them.

Max and his friends knew they couldn't keep running and decided to face the shadow. They turned around and saw that the shadow was now right in front of them.

It was a terrifying monster, with glowing eyes and sharp claws. Max and his friends froze in shock as the monster began to circle them.

But then Max remembered something he had read in a book. He knew that the monster was afraid of fire. He took a flashlight from his backpack and flipped the switch. A bright beam of light illuminated the darkness of the forest and the monster flinched.

Max and his friends took the chance and ran as fast as they could. The shadow no longer pursued them, and they finally reached home safely.

From that day on, they knew that the dark forest was full of secrets and scary creatures. But they were ready to face whatever would come their way.

THE MYSTERIOUS CASE of the missing school bus

It was a normal day for the students of Friedrich Kraus Elementary School until the school bus that was supposed to take them home disappeared. The children waited and waited, but the bus never came.

The children's parents were worried and alerted the police. A big search was launched, but there was no trace of the bus or the children.

Max and his friends decided to investigate on their own. They had an idea where the bus could be and set off.

When they arrived at the abandoned train station, they saw a mysterious man loitering near the station. He looked like he was hiding something.

The children decided to follow him and saw him open a secret door that led to an underground room. The room was full of cobwebs and darkness, but they could see the missing school bus.

Suddenly they heard footsteps, and the mysterious man appeared. He was the bus driver! He had kidnapped the children and taken them to the underground room to extort ransom from their parents.

Max and his friends knew they had to act quickly. They used their flashlights to blind the man and managed to free the children from the bus.

The police were called and the bus driver was arrested. The children were rescued and returned safely to their parents.

From that day on, they knew that sometimes it was necessary to investigate on their own and be brave to save their friends.

THE UNCANNY ENCOUNTER with a vampire

It was a dark and stormy night when Max and his friends were on their way home from an afternoon in the park. Suddenly, they heard a strange noise behind them. It sounded like whispering, getting closer and closer.

The children turned around and saw a mysterious man in a cape coming toward them. He had sharp teeth and was looking at them with his red eyes.

Max and his friends immediately realized that they were facing a vampire. They ran as fast as they could, but the vampire always seemed to be one step ahead of them.

They hid in an old shed, but the vampire quickly found them. They tried to fight him off, but he was too strong for them.

Just as the vampire was about to pounce on Max, a bright beam of light appeared. It was the glow of the rising sun. The vampire quickly fled into the darkness, and Max and his friends were saved.

They knew they had been lucky, but they were also glad to know that they were now prepared if they ever encountered another vampire.

From that day on, they remembered that courage and cohesion are the best protection against the scary creatures of the night.

THE MYSTERY OF THE old cemetery

One sunny afternoon, Max and his friends decided to explore the old cemetery, which had been abandoned for years. They had heard that it was supposedly haunted, but they didn't really believe it.

When they entered the cemetery, they quickly realized that something was wrong. The graves looked like they had just been dug, but there were no workers or activity in the cemetery. It was also very quiet, no birds chirping or other sounds.

They continued to wander when suddenly they heard a noise. It sounded like a soft whisper. They followed the sound and found a group of ghostly figures standing around a grave.

One of the ghosts seemed to be walking toward Max. Max and his friends ran away, but the ghost followed them. They knew they had to escape before it was too late.

They found an old abandoned tower and climbed in to hide. They heard the ghost coming closer, but then suddenly it became very quiet.

When they dared to look out, they saw the ghost disappear and realized that it was just an illusion. They discovered an old book that explained the mystery of the cemetery.

It turned out that the ghosts were the guards of the cemetery to make sure that no mischief came to the cemetery. Max and his friends understood that it was important to respect and honor the cemetery and went home with a new understanding of life and death.

THE GHOST HUNTERS IN the abandoned factory

Max and his friends had heard about an abandoned factory that was supposedly haunted by ghosts. They decided to dress up as ghost hunters and explore the factory.

When they arrived, they quickly realized that something was wrong. The factory was completely dark and silent. They started creeping through the empty corridors when suddenly they heard a noise.

They followed the sound and found a group of ghosts standing around an old machine. Max and his friends quickly realized that the ghosts were from the machines in the factory.

They decided to solve the mystery of the ghosts and find the origin of their apparitions. They climbed on the machine and began to examine it.

Suddenly, the machine began to rattle and hum, and max and his friends were hit by an eerie electric shock. They fainted and when they woke up, they were in a room with the ghosts.

They learned that the ghosts were former workers who worked on the machine before an unfortunate accident killed them. Their spirits remained trapped in the factory and had been trying to get the machine system working again ever since.

Max and his friends decided to help the ghosts by repairing the machine system. They managed to get the machine working again, and the ghosts were released and could finally find peace.

The ghost hunters had successfully uncovered a ghost story and with their help restored peace to the ghosts. They left the factory with a new understanding of the power of technology and the spirit world.

THE SPOOKY STORY OF the ghost train

A strange thing is happening at the Willow Creek train station. A train that hasn't run in years seems to be rolling down the tracks again. But as people approach, they find that the train has no driver and all the windows of the train cars are blacked out. Some say they hear strange noises coming from the train, as if someone is inside. The locals have been telling each other the story of the ghost train that crashed on the track for years.

Of course, the local kids don't believe the story, until one night one of them decides to take a closer look at the ghost train. But as he approaches the train, he starts screaming and runs away. The other children rush to him and find him lying unconscious on the ground. He has seen a creepy shadow coming from the train.

When the children decide to get to the bottom of the mystery, they discover that the train is not only cursed, but also possessed by a dangerous spirit. Together with an old train guard, they try to banish the ghost and bring the train to a halt for good. Will they manage to stop the ghost train and unravel the mystery of its origin?

THE EERIE DISAPPEARANCE of the neighbor

One day, the neighborhood children notice that their neighbor, Mr. Petersen, has disappeared. His car is still in front of the house, but there is no sign that he is still there. The children begin to investigate and discover that Mr. Petersen has been acting strangely lately. He has had constant visits from creepy characters and his curtains have always been drawn.

The children decide to investigate Mr. Petersen's house and find evidence that he may have been kidnapped. As they look around further, they discover a secret room in the basement that is full of strange objects. On a table in the middle of the room is an old box with a lock on it. The children feel that they have found an important clue here and decide to pick the lock.

But when they open the box, something eerie happens: a cold mist rises from the box and a ghostly shadow appears, quickly spreading in all directions. The children are caught by it and pulled into another world, where they meet eerie creatures and strange spirits.

The children must now summon all their courage to free themselves from this world and save Mr. Petersen. With the help of brave decisions and the support of their friends, they find out who is behind the disappearance of their neighbor and what the strange box is all about. Will they succeed in defeating the kidnappers and bringing Mr. Petersen back home?

The cursed mask of the carnival

It was a week before the carnival and the city was in full celebratory mood. People were preparing their costumes and the streets were decorated with colorful decorations. Mia and her friends Lisa and Tom were also excited and planning their own costume. But they had no idea that they would soon make a scary discovery.

One day, while strolling through the streets, they discovered an old junk store that had a large selection of carnival masks. As they entered the store, they noticed an eerie mask that looked different from all the others. It was a gold mask with sparkling gems and carved designs. Mia was fascinated by the mask and decided to buy it.

When she put the mask on, she immediately sensed that something was wrong. An eerie feeling came over her and she could feel her skin ripple into goosebumps. But she pushed her fears aside and decided to wear the mask at the carnival.

On the night of the carnival, she and her friends paraded through the streets and celebrated exuberantly. But when Mia wore the mask, strange things began to happen. She felt someone or something following her and heard an eerie whispering in her ears. When she pointed it out to her friends, they just laughed and said it was just her imagination.

But later that night, as they were on their way home, a mysterious man suddenly appeared and said, "Give me back my mask!" Before they could react, the man disappeared just as quickly as he had appeared. Mia and her friends were shocked and scared.

They decided to get rid of the mask and took it back to the junk store. But when they entered the store, an even bigger surprise awaited them. The shopkeeper had disappeared and in his place stood an eerie figure in a black cloak. The figure demanded the mask back and warned them of the consequences if they did not return it.

Mia and her friends knew they had to act before it was too late. They decided to destroy the mask and planned a scheme. The next day they returned to the store and destroyed the mask with a hammer.

From that day on, the town was never haunted by eerie events again and the friends knew that they had saved the town from a dark force. Mia and her friends were relieved that it was all over, but they also knew that they would have to stay ever vigilant in case evil should appear again.

THE MYSTERIOUS CASE of the missing treasure

It was a sunny day and the children of the local treasure hunt club were out for a new adventure. This time they had found an old map that would lead to a hidden treasure. The kids were excited and ready to do anything to find the treasure.

They followed the map and eventually came to an old abandoned mansion on the outskirts of town. The mansion was old and dilapidated and had a creepy, spooky charm. The children decided to explore the building, hoping to find clues to the treasure.

They walked through the dilapidated door and found themselves in a large, dusty room. There was nothing but a huge mirror on the wall. Suddenly they noticed a strange inscription on the mirror that they had not noticed before.

It read, "The treasure is hidden here, but you must awaken it with the blood of a victim."

The children were frightened and did not know what to do. They were sure that they did not want to find a treasure at the expense of a sacrifice. They decided to leave the building and give the map to the police.

However, when they were outside, they noticed that one of their friends, Max, was missing. They searched the building again and finally found him in a secret room, where he was being held captive by a mysterious figure.

It was a man who introduced himself as the original owner of the property. He had left the mansion to search for gold, but when he returned, he found that his wife had betrayed him and stolen the treasure. Since then, he has guarded the building to make sure no one finds his treasure.

The children were brave and smart and managed to free Max and find the treasure without having to make a sacrifice. They overpowered the man and handed him over to the police.

At the end of the day, the children were tired but happy and proud of themselves. They had had another adventure and found a treasure without anyone getting hurt.

The scary encounter with a werewolf

Tim and his friends, Emma and Max, were on their way home from school when they suddenly saw a strange figure in the forest. It was tall and had furry ears, and it seemed to walk on two legs. It moved quickly and elegantly, but it was hard to tell exactly what it was.

"What is that?" asked Emma as they watched the eerie creature.

"I think it's a werewolf!" whispered Max, who, being a big horror movie fan, immediately recognized the resemblance.

"A werewolf? Is there really such a thing?" asked Tim skeptically, but he couldn't deny that he also had a queasy feeling.

They decided to follow the creature to find out what it was up to. They eventually came to a small clearing where they saw it turn into a man, who approached them.

"Sorry if I startled you," the man said, "I am a werewolf, but I do not harm humans. I am looking for a cure for my curse."

The children were relieved when they realized that the werewolf was friendly and did not want to harm them. They told him about their adventures and told him how they had encountered other creatures as well.

"Maybe you can help me find the cure," said the werewolf, "I know you have had many adventures and you are brave enough to help me."

The children agreed and began their search for the cure. They searched forests, caves and creepy old houses until they finally found a mysterious potion that could help the werewolf.

They returned to the werewolf and gave him the potion, which helped him turn back into a normal man.

"Thank you so much for helping me," said the man, "I will never forget you and I will always remember your friendship."

The children said goodbye to their new friend and went home. They were proud of themselves for being able to help a creature in need, and they didn't let their creepiness stop them either. It was an adventure they would never forget.

THE MYSTERIOUS CASE of the haunted house

The siblings, Max and Anna, were curious and adventurous. One sunny day, as they were taking a walk around the town, they noticed an old abandoned house on the outskirts of the town. The house looked very creepy and it seemed like it had been abandoned for years. The windows were all broken and the roof looked like it was going to collapse at any moment. Max and Anna were intrigued by the creepy house and decided to take a closer look.

As they got closer, they suddenly heard a strange noise, as if someone was walking around the house. The siblings became more curious and decided to enter the house. They climbed over the fence and sneaked inside through the broken door.

Inside, it was dark and quiet. Max and Anna looked around and noticed that the house was full of dust and cobwebs. Suddenly, they heard the sound of footsteps again. This time it came from upstairs. Max and Anna decided to go up the stairs to see what was going on.

When they reached the top floor, they saw an old room filled with furniture and boxes. But the strange thing was that everything was covered with a thick dust, except for one chair, which looked strangely clean. Max and Anna approached the chair and suddenly noticed that it was moving. Then they saw something that made their blood run cold.

A creepy, transparent face suddenly appeared in front of them, with white hair and green eyes that glowed in the darkness. It seemed as if the face wanted to scream, but it could not make a sound. Max and Anna were filled with panic and ran out of the house as fast as they could.

When they were outside, they noticed that the house suddenly changed. It no longer looked old and abandoned, but new and neat. They looked back and saw that the creepy face in the window had disappeared.

The siblings didn't know what they had seen, but they knew they would never return to the house. They went home and told their parents about their spooky adventure in the haunted house. But no one believed them.

The spooky haunting at school

It was a normal school day when suddenly strange things started happening in the school. Doors opened and closed on their own, books flew through the air, and there were eerie sounds coming from the empty classrooms.

The students were worried and confused. They wondered what was going on. The teachers tried to reassure them by telling them that it was just the wind or that the building was old and making strange noises.

But it couldn't be. There was no wind and the noises were too loud to be coming from an old building. The children began to wonder and decided to get to the bottom of it.

One afternoon they decided to stay at school and investigate the haunting. They took flashlights and walked through the hallways. Suddenly, they heard a noise coming from the classroom down the hall. When they went inside, they discovered it was the classroom where a student had died years ago.

Suddenly they heard a voice telling them to leave. They looked around and saw no one. But they sensed that something was wrong. Then they saw a figure standing at the window. It could only be described as a ghost.

The children were frightened and ran out of the room. They decided to inform their teachers and parents about what had happened. Together with them they returned, but there was nothing to be seen.

From that day on, the children were more careful when they were at school. They were careful not to stay alone in the school and were always on the lookout for strange happenings.

The school was later renovated and there have been no reports of the spooky haunting since. However, the students still told each other the story of the ghost and what they had experienced. It was a story that would never be forgotten.

THE GHOSTLY ENCOUNTER in the library

The library was a quiet place full of knowledge and mystery. But that night, everything was about to change. Sophie and her friends Emma and Ben had met at the library to work on a school project. As they sat in the quiet hall, they suddenly heard a strange whisper. It sounded almost like a voice coming from an old book.

Sophie hesitated, but then she got up and went to the bookshelf. She had the feeling that someone or something was staring at her. As she took a book from the shelf, an old map suddenly fell to the floor. The map showed the layout of the library, but there was a room they had never seen before.

"Oh, my God!" whispered Emma, pointing to the map. "I have a feeling this is a hidden room."

Sophie was drawn to the idea of finding a hidden room and decided to investigate the map. She led the group through the library and eventually found a door that was on an old shelf.

The room behind it was dusty and old. There were a lot of books and boxes scattered everywhere. But Sophie immediately noticed that something was wrong. The temperature in the room was a lot colder than in the library and she couldn't shake the feeling that they weren't alone.

Then they noticed a shadow moving on the wall. "What is that?" asked Ben, pointing at the shadow. "Maybe it's just the light," Emma suggested, but Sophie knew it was something else.

As they approached the shadow, they suddenly heard the whispering again. This time it was louder and more distinct. It almost sounded like a plea for help.

Sophie, Emma and Ben became nervous and decided to leave the room. But when they turned around, they noticed that the door was locked behind them. They were trapped!

They heard the whispering louder and louder and it almost seemed as if they were surrounded by many voices. Suddenly a little girl appeared in an old dress they had never seen before.

"Can you help me?" the girl asked with a sad look. "I've been locked in here and I can't get out."

Sophie, Emma and Ben decided to help the girl and looked for a way out. After some time, they found an old box with a key inside. With the key they were able to open the door and free the girl.

"Thank you for helping me," the girl said and then suddenly disappeared into thin air. Sophie, Emma and Ben were stunned and amazed, but they knew they had just had a ghostly encounter in the library.

The legend of the creepy haunted castle

Lena and Max were excited. They were on their way to an old castle that they had heard was haunted by ghosts. The stories they had heard were disturbing and creepy. But that didn't stop the two adventurers from visiting the castle and seeing if the legends were true.

When they arrived, they saw that the castle looked old and dilapidated. The windows were broken and the door creaked when they opened it. Inside it was dark and eerie, but Lena and Max bravely crept on.

They went up the stairs and entered a room with a large fireplace. Suddenly they heard a noise and when they turned around, they saw that the door had closed behind them. Lena and Max were trapped!

They heard footsteps and ghostly voices whispering, "You will never escape." Lena and Max became frightened. But then they saw a figure in the darkness. It was a ghost that appeared to them.

The ghost told them the legend of the castle: many years ago, a count had lived here. He was cruel and had people tortured and murdered in his dungeons. When he died, his ghost was trapped in the castle.

Since then he haunted the castle and his soul was restless. But the ghost had a request for Lena and Max. They should find the key to the dungeons and free him. Then his soul could finally rest.

Lena and Max were nervous, but they decided to help the ghost. They searched the castle and finally found the key in an old hiding place. They ran to the dungeons and opened the door. The ghost was free!

They saw the ghost vanish into thin air and felt a sense of relief when they realized they could safely leave the castle. They ran out of the castle and into the sun.

Since then, they have never heard from the ghost again. But they will never forget how they entered the castle and released the ghost.

THE MYSTERIOUS DISAPPEARANCE of the student

It was a sunny day and all the students were excited for the upcoming school project. But when the student Lena didn't show up, the excitement was quickly replaced by concern. Teachers immediately began searching and scoured the entire school grounds, but Lena was nowhere to be found.

The police were called and soon the students and teachers joined the search teams. They combed the forest and all the surrounding areas, but there was no sign of Lena. When night fell, everyone was exhausted and desperate.

The next day there was a shocking discovery. A little girl who lived near the school had observed something strange. She testified that she had seen Lena accompanied by a man who had pulled her into a car.

Police immediately began searching for the car and the man. After intensive investigation and questioning, the man was finally found. It turned out that he was a criminal who had kidnapped the girl to extort ransom.

Thanks to the quick response of the police and the cooperation of the students and teachers, Lena was saved. The student was scared but unharmed and safe.

The students and teachers were relieved and grateful that Lena was found. But they were also shocked at how close to the crime had happened at the school. They realized how important it was to always be alert and vigilant and to protect each other.

The eerie haunting of the cemetery

The night was dark and foggy when Finn and his friends went to the local cemetery. It was a spooky place they didn't usually go, but they had heard it was haunted.

They crept through the old graves, keeping an eye out for anything unexplained. Suddenly, they heard a soft whisper and the rattling of chains. They followed the sound and discovered a figure wrapped in a white robe with chains around its wrists.

Finn and his friends froze in shock as the figure approached them. They had never seen anything like it before and didn't know what to do. The figure came closer and closer and they could hear the plaintive moans coming from its mouth.

Suddenly they realized that it must be the ghost of a woman who had been buried in the cemetery a long time ago. She seemed to be looking for something and reached out her chains to touch Finn and his friends.

Finn and his friends ran for their lives and left the cemetery in a hurry. They had enough of that creepy place and promised themselves never to return there again.

The next day they decided to visit the local historian and ask him about the history of the cemetery. They learned that the cemetery had been used as an execution site many years ago and that there were many unfortunate souls there who could not find peace.

Finn and his friends decided to help the woman's spirit by looking for her grave and decorating it with flowers. They hoped that this would help her finally find peace.

From that day on, they were still afraid of the cemetery, but they knew they had done something good. And who knows, maybe the next time they visited the cemetery they wouldn't be so afraid.

THE MYSTERIOUS ENCOUNTER in the old villa

It was a sunny day when the five friends, Emma, Tim, Mia, Tom and Lisa decided to take a trip to an old mansion that had been abandoned for years. It was a mysterious and creepy house that still had many stories and secrets to tell.

When they entered the house, they immediately felt an eerie atmosphere. The furniture was covered in dust, the wallpaper was peeling, and the windows were covered in cobwebs. The friends began to explore the house and soon found a room with a large, heavy door that was locked.

Curious and fascinated by the door, they decided to find out what was hiding behind it. With their combined efforts, they finally managed to open the door. What they saw took their breath away. A long, gloomy room with a large desk and an old book lying open on it.

They approached the book and began to read it. Suddenly they heard a noise and a figure in a long black coat appeared in front of them. It was a ghostly creature that looked like a man, but was transparent. The friends were frightened and ran out of the room.

When they were outside, they wondered what they had just seen. Was it really a ghost or just their imagination? They decided to go to town and find out more about the mansion and its history.

They found out that the owner of the mansion had died many years ago and that since then many people had reported eerie happenings in the house. They also learned about a secret room that the owner always kept locked, where he kept his most valuable treasures.

The friends returned to the mansion and began to search for the secret room. They searched the whole house until they finally discovered a hidden room filled with valuable treasures.

When they left the room, they heard the sound again and the figure in the long black coat appeared in front of them again. But this time they were not startled. They now knew that it was the spirit of the owner, who only wanted to warn them about the dangers of the treasures.

The friends decided to leave the treasures in the room and leave the house. They had enough adventure and creepiness for one day. As they made their way back, they knew they had a story to tell that they would never forget.

The spooky story of being haunted in the hospital

Night was falling as Tim and his friends, Lisa and Max, stood outside the old hospital. It was a gloomy and abandoned place that had not been in operation for years. The windows were cracked, the door was stuck, and the sign that said "Hospital" hung crookedly on the wall.

"We shouldn't be here," Lisa whispered in a shaky voice. "It's dangerous and scary."

"Oh, come on," Max countered, "We're ghost hunters. We're not afraid of any spooky creatures."

But as they entered the hospital, they felt an eerie chill settle into their bodies. The hallway was dark and deserted, but somewhere they heard a noise. It sounded like the rattling of doors or the pounding of footsteps on the floor.

They followed the sound and eventually found themselves in an old hospital room. On the bed was a strange object. It was an old hospital mask stained with blood.

Suddenly they heard the breathing of a being they could not see. They sensed that something was near them, but when they turned around, there was nothing. Then they heard a voice whispering, "Go away before it's too late."

Tim, Lisa and Max ran out of the hospital and never returned. They didn't tell anyone about the creepy haunting at the hospital, but they knew there was something supernatural there. Something they would never forget.

THE MYSTERIOUS CASE of the missing child

The sun had already set and the moon was shining brightly in the sky when the ghost hunters were called to a new case. This time it was about a missing child named Max, who had disappeared without a trace for days.

The ghost hunters made their way to Max's house to question his parents. The mother burst into tears as she told them about her missing son. She told them that Max often played alone in the nearby playground and that she missed him. They had already called the police, but so far there was no trace of Max.

The ghost hunters decided to investigate the playground and started their search. Suddenly, they heard a strange whispering that seemed to come from a nearby bush. They cautiously approached the bushes and discovered a mysterious figure hiding behind the bushes. It was a strange man with a long coat and a hat, who was acting suspiciously.

The ghost hunters decided to follow the man to find out if he had something to do with Max's disappearance. They followed him to an old abandoned house on the outskirts of town. When they entered the house, they noticed that it was full of cobwebs and dust, as if it had been abandoned for years.

Suddenly they heard the crying of a child from one of the rooms. They rushed into the room and found Max sitting on a chair, bound and gagged. He was scared and relieved when he saw the ghost hunters.

The Ghostbusters freed Max and took him back to his parents. However, the suspicious man escaped and was never caught. The ghost hunters suspected that he was involved in dark dealings and that they still had a lot to find out about him.

Max was finally back home and his parents were happy to hold him in their arms. The ghost hunters had once again solved a case, but there were many more adventures waiting for them.

The eerie encounter with a witch

It was a dark and foggy night when the friends Emma, Max and Leo were on their way home. Suddenly they heard a strange noise and saw a figure in the distance. It was an old woman with a crooked back and long, shaggy hair standing in front of them.

She had a black hat on her head and was wearing a dark robe. The children froze in fear as the old woman looked at them with her piercing eyes. "What are you doing here?" she asked in a smoky tone.

The children stammered to themselves and explained that they were on their way home. But the old woman did not believe them and said, "You have taken the wrong road, children. Follow me and I will take you back."

The children hesitated, but they were afraid that they were lost. So they followed the old woman. But as they got closer to her, they sensed an eerie energy around them.

The old woman led them to an abandoned house on the outskirts of town. The children hesitated, but the woman said, "Go inside and I will show you the way."

When they entered the house, a surprise awaited them. The room was full of magic books, herbs and other strange objects. In the middle of the room stood a witch with a huge cauldron in which a green liquid was bubbling.

The children froze in horror. The witch laughed loudly and said, "You have come just in time. I need three children to make my potion."

The children realized they were in great danger and fled the house. The witch and the old woman ran after them, but the children were faster and managed to escape.

They ran as fast as they could back to town and told the police about their encounter with the witch. The police investigated the abandoned house but found no one there.

Since then, the children of the town have been telling each other the spooky story of their scary encounter with the witch.

THE CURSED STATUE IN the church

Mia and Max are on their way to the church to do a school assignment. They are supposed to give a presentation about the history of the church. However, when they get there, the church is locked. They see an old man nearby who tells them that the church has been closed for years and that no one is allowed to enter. Mia and Max are curious and decide to enter the church to investigate.

When they break open the door, they see a statue in the middle of the room. The statue looks like a character from a horror movie and the kids get nervous. Suddenly, they hear strange noises and see shadows flitting around the room. The children are frightened and want to escape, but the door is now locked.

They look for a way out and discover a hidden room behind the statue. There they find an old document that says the statue is cursed and anyone who touches it is damned.

The children are desperate and don't know what to do. Suddenly they hear a noise and see a ghost coming towards them. They close their eyes and expect the worst, but when they look up again, the ghost has disappeared.

They decide to leave the church and take the certificate with them to inform their teacher. When they are outside, they see that the old man has disappeared. They are not sure if he helped them or if he has something to do with the curse.

Mia and Max decide to break the curse of the statue and return to the church. They touch the statue and say a prayer. Suddenly, the statue begins to glow and the curse is broken.

The children are relieved and happy that they have broken the curse. They return to school and tell their teacher about their adventure. The teacher is impressed by their courage and gives them an A for their paper. Mia and Max are proud of themselves and know that they can do anything if they stick together.

The mysterious haunting of the old factory

It was a cold and windy day in the fall when Tim, Hannah, and Max decided to explore the old factory on the outskirts of town. The factory had been abandoned for years and was rumored to be haunted. The kids were excited about the idea and decided to go in search of ghosts.

When they entered the factory, they immediately noticed the musty smell. There were old machines and tools lying around everywhere, and the walls were covered in dust and cobwebs. They were in a large room when suddenly a door behind them slammed shut and would not open.

The children became frightened and began to look for a way to get out of the room. They heard footsteps, but when they turned around, they saw no one. Suddenly it started to flicker and they heard an eerie laughter. They got scared and started running.

They ran around the factory floor, but it seemed like they were going in circles. They kept seeing the same machines and equipment. Suddenly they heard a loud noise and when they turned around they saw a shadow on the wall.

They ran faster than ever and finally came to a door that they could open. They ran down the hall and opened another door. They stood in a small room and saw a strange figure with a creepy laugh in front of them.

They ran and finally managed to escape from the factory. They breathed a sigh of relief and decided never to go back to the old factory.

Later, when they talked about it with their friends, one of them told them that there had been a terrible accident in the factory many years ago. Since then, it was reported that it was haunted. The children were glad that they had escaped and vowed never to do anything like that again.

THE SPOOKY STORY OF the cursed forest.

Friends Max, Lisa and Tim are in search of the mysterious treasure of the forest. They have heard that there is an old tree in the forest that shows the way to the treasure. However, the forest is considered cursed and no one dares to enter.

Nevertheless, the three friends dare the adventure and set off into the forest. As they walk deeper into the forest, they sense an eerie silence and an oppressive atmosphere. The forest seems to be alive, and the trees seem as if they are blocking the friends' way.

Suddenly, they hear a strange cracking and rustling sound. A dark figure emerges from the shadow of a tree. It is an old, wizened creature with deep eye sockets and dirty fingernails. It wears tattered clothes and reeks of decay.

The friends froze in fear and could not get a word out. The creature began to speak, in a smoky, hoarse voice that seemed to come from deep in its throat. "You have entered the cursed forest," it said, "There is no salvation for you here. You will remain here forever."

The friends didn't know what to do when suddenly they saw a glow of light at the end of the path. They realized that it was the tree that showed the way to the treasure. Without hesitation, they ran, pursued by the creepy creature.

When they reached the tree, they realized that it was indeed pointing the way to the treasure. The friends followed the directions and eventually found the treasure. But when they turned around, the hooded creature was standing in front of them.

They quickly grabbed the treasure and ran as fast as they could. Behind them they heard the creature screaming and cursing. But they were not stopped and managed to escape from the cursed forest.

When they were sure they were outside the forest, they took a closer look at the treasure. It was an old chest filled with gold and jewels. They laughed with joy and relief at their adventure.

But they agreed that they would never return to the cursed forest. For who knows what else might have been waiting for them.

The mysterious disappearance of the teacher

There is great excitement in the class of Tim and his friends. The teacher, Mr. Müller, has not been to class for days. Nobody knows where he is. Even the police have not found any clues yet.

One day, Tim and his friends decide to get to the bottom of the matter. They break into the abandoned house where Mr. Müller was last seen. It is dark and eerie in the old walls. Dusty furniture is everywhere and cobwebs hang from the ceiling. Suddenly they hear a noise. It sounds like a groan and comes from the cellar.

The friends bravely make their way there. They open the door and stand in front of a spiral staircase that leads down into the depths. The steps are rusted and rotten, but the friends put one foot in front of the other and descend. At the bottom of the stairs, they see a door that is open a crack.

Slowly and carefully they enter and find themselves in a small room. In the middle is an old desk on which lies a photograph of Mr. Müller. He is bound and gagged and looks very scared. Next to it is a small note that says, "If you want to see the teacher again, you must do the tasks I give you."

Suddenly, the lights go out and the door slams shut. The friends are trapped and don't know what to do. But then they hear a voice coming from the darkness. It is Mr. Müller! He is tied up, but he can speak. He tells the children that he was kidnapped by a former student who wanted to play a trick on him.

Together, the friends manage to get out of the bondage and free the teacher. They take him to the police and the student is caught and punished. The teacher is saved and the friends have once again proven that they are a great team.

THE GHOSTLY ENCOUNTER at the cinema

It was a chilly evening in October and the children were excited because today was the day of the premiere of the latest scary movie at the cinema. When they bought the tickets, they noticed that they were the only customers.

The group of kids thought this was a little strange, but they were too excited to notice. When the movie began, they sat spellbound as the spooky plot unfolded. But then, during one of the scary scenes, something strange happened. Suddenly, the projector went off and the lights in the theater went out.

The children were sitting in complete darkness when suddenly they heard a strange whisper. It seemed to come from nowhere and became louder and louder. Then the lights came back on and the children looked around and realized that they were not alone in the movie theater.

They saw a figure in an old, worn movie costume standing on the screen. The figure slowly turned around and looked directly at the children. The children were frightened and tried to escape, but the doors of the movie theater were locked.

The figure on the screen began to move and the children saw that it seemed to step out of the picture. Then the figure became clearer and the children realized that it was a ghost. A ghost that was apparently looking for someone.

The children stood paralyzed as the ghost approached them. But then, as he stood right in front of them, he suddenly disappeared and the movie theater was empty again.

The kids rushed out of the movie theater when it finally opened and told the operator their scary story. But when he checked the surveillance cameras, he couldn't find anything unusual.

Was it really just their imagination, or had they really had a ghostly encounter in the movie theater? The kids didn't know, but they were sure they would never watch a scary movie in the theater again.

The spooky encounter with a zombie

The sun was slowly setting, turning the sky a deep red. The streets were empty and silent. Only the crackling of leaves being blown by the wind could be heard.

The three friends, Emma, Tom and Lena, had decided to go to the abandoned park on the outskirts of the city. When they got there, they noticed something strange. The park was completely silent and deserted. There were no birds, no squirrels, and no people. It was almost as if the park was dead.

While they were strolling through the park, they suddenly heard a strange noise. It sounded like the crunching of bones and the moaning of an eerie creature.

The friends began to walk faster, but the sound grew louder and louder. Suddenly, a dark shadow emerged from the bushes. It was a zombie!

The zombie threw its head back and let out a terrible scream. Emma, Tom and Lena froze in fear. The zombie came closer and closer. But then suddenly they screamed together and ran away.

They ran and ran until they reached the exit of the park. The zombie was not far behind them, but they managed to escape from him.

When they arrived home, they told their parents about the scary event. However, no one believed them. But the friends knew what they had seen. They were sure that the zombie was still up to his mischief in the park and was ready to wait for his next victims.

The spooky story of the cursed river

The sun was just about to set when the friends Mia, Tom and Emma arrived at the river. They were going on a night hike to see the cursed river they had heard so much about. The river was known for its dark history and the many unexplained events that had taken place there.

The friends were following the path along the river when suddenly they heard a strange noise. It sounded like an eerie whisper that seemed to come from the river itself. They looked around, but there was no one to be seen.

Suddenly it became cold and the sky darkened. An eerie figure appeared in front of them. It was a woman who looked like a witch, with disheveled hair and a long black coat. The friends froze in fear. The witch began to speak, but her words were unintelligible. It seemed as if she spoke in an ancient language.

The friends tried to escape, but the witch followed them. She moved quickly and was all around them. She cast a curse on the friends and they could not move. They were trapped and could not escape.

The witch began to tell a scary story, about a man who had fallen into the river many years ago and was cursed to stay in it and steal the soul of anyone who got too close. The friends were trembling with fear and could not believe what they were hearing.

Suddenly the witch disappeared and the friends were free. They ran as fast as they could until they arrived home safely. They were exhausted and scared, but they knew they would never be near the river again.

From that day on, the cursed river was a place they would only look at from a distance. The creepy story of the witch and the cursed man would always remain in their memories.

The mysterious case of the kidnapped child

Lena and Max were sitting on the bench in the park, enjoying the warm sun. Suddenly they heard screaming and a woman ran towards them.

"Please, help me! My son has been kidnapped!" she cried desperately.

Lena and Max immediately jumped up and followed the woman. She led them to an old warehouse on the outskirts of town. When they arrived, they saw a man with a child in his hand disappearing into the warehouse.

"That's him! That's the man who kidnapped my son!" the woman screamed.

Lena and Max didn't hesitate for a moment and ran after the man. They struggled through the dark hallways looking for the child. Suddenly they heard crying and followed the sound.

They found the child in a room, but before they could free him, the kidnapper appeared. He held a gun in his hand and threatened to shoot them if they moved.

Lena and Max were in great danger when suddenly a police car arrived in front of the warehouse. The police officers rushed into the building and were able to overpower the kidnapper and free the child.

Lena and Max were praised for their brave act and honored by the police for their help in solving the case.

"We're glad we were able to help," Lena said.

"Yes, it was an exciting experience, but we are glad that everything turned out well," Max added.

The two friends went home happy and relieved, knowing they had acted in a difficult situation when it mattered.

THE GHOSTLY ENCOUNTER at the museum

It was a sunny day when the friends visited the museum. They had already seen many exhibitions and were excited by the stories they learned. But suddenly they felt an eerie atmosphere. It was as if they were being watched.

When they turned around, they saw a ghost! He was floating through the corridors of the museum and seemed to be looking for something. The friends were scared, but also curious. They decided to follow the ghost and find out what he was looking for.

They followed him through the museum and finally came to an exhibit about Egyptian mummies. There they saw that the ghost was pointing to a particular mummy. The friends approached cautiously and noticed that the mummy had a mysterious curse.

Suddenly, they heard a noise and turned around. Another group of visitors had come and noticed the ghost and the friends. They were laughing and making fun of the friends.

But then something incredible happened: the ghost turned into a powerful wizard! He expelled the other visitors to the museum and told the friends that he would send them on a dangerous mission to break the curse and save the mummy.

The friends agreed and were given magical powers. They set out and crossed dangerous deserts and ancient pyramids. Finally, they found the mummy's secret tomb and broke the curse.

When they returned to the museum, they were greeted as heroes and the wizard thanked them for their bravery. The friends said their goodbyes, knowing that this was an adventure they would never forget.

The uncanny encounter with a demon

Evil lurks in the darkness. Max and his friends had to experience this firsthand. They had hidden in an abandoned house to play the game "Werewolf". But suddenly they felt an eerie presence in the room. They could sense that something evil was in the air.

The light flickered and a dark figure appeared in Front of them. It was a demon, staring at them with red eyes, intimidating them with its malevolent presence. Max and his friends were paralyzed and did not know what to do. But then they were jolted out of their torpor by a brave voice.

It was Max's little sister Lilly, who rushed to help. She had heard about the game and was curious. Without hesitation, she confronted the demon. The demon seemed surprised by her fearlessness and hesitated for a moment.

But then he attacked her. Max and his friends screamed in horror as the demon grabbed Lilly and disappeared into the darkness. They knew they had to save her, but how?

In desperation, they decided to turn to the old history books they had found in the library. They hoped to find a solution to their problem there. There they came across an ancient spell that could defeat demons. It was risky, but it was their only chance.

With trembling hands, they began to recite the spell to defeat the demon. Suddenly, they felt an immense power in their bodies that they had never experienced before. The room filled with a bright flash of light, and when they looked around again, the demon was gone. Lilly had been saved.

Max and his friends hugged Lilly happily, rejoicing that they had succeeded in their adventure. But they also knew that they had to be more careful in the future and never feel too safe. Evil lurked everywhere and could strike at any time.

THE CURSED SCROLL IN the temple

It was a sunny day when Mia and Tom decided to visit the temple on the outskirts of the city. The temple was known for its ancient history and the cursed scroll that was kept inside. The scroll was passed down from generation to generation and was said to contain a powerful curse.

When Mia and Tom entered the temple, they immediately felt a strange energy flowing through the room. They saw the scroll on a pedestal in the middle of the room and felt an eerie presence around them. They decided to step closer to examine the scroll more closely.

But when they touched the scroll, something strange happened. The scroll suddenly began to glow and a dark mist filled the room. Out of the mist appeared a figure that Mia and Tom first thought was a priest. But as the figure got closer, they realized it was a demon!

The demon laughed wickedly and said that he was reclaiming the scroll that had been kept in this temple for many centuries. But Mia and Tom refused to give the scroll to the demon. They knew they had to do something to defeat the demon and break the curse.

They bravely faced the demon and fought with all their strength. It was a long and difficult battle, but finally Mia and Tom managed to defeat the demon and save the scroll.

As they carefully placed the scroll on the ground, they felt relief and a strange warmth coursing through their bodies. They knew that the curse was broken and that they could safely leave the temple.

Mia and Tom walked out of the temple and looked back once more. They knew they had accomplished a dangerous task today, but they were glad they had. They had proven that they were brave and strong and that they could win any battle if they just stuck together.

THE MYSTERIOUS HAUNTING of the old castle

The sun had set and night was falling as Tim, Lina and Max approached the old castle. They had heard that the abandoned walls were haunted, and they wanted to find out if it was really true.

The castle was huge and gloomy, and as the children got closer, they heard a low whimpering sound that seemed to come from inside the castle. They decided that they really had to find out what was going on there.

Cautiously, they entered the castle and crept through the dark corridors and rooms. They heard strange noises and felt they were being watched, but they couldn't see anything.

Suddenly they heard a loud moaning coming from one of the rooms. As they got closer, they saw a figure in chains in front of them, looking at them with a blank stare. It was a ghost!

The children froze in fright, but then Tim overcame his fear and stepped closer. The ghost began to speak and told them the story of the castle. Many years ago a terrible crime had taken place here and since then the ghost of the victim had haunted the walls of the castle.

The children felt sorry for the ghost and decided to help him find peace. They searched for the perpetrator's hiding place and found a scroll that incriminated him.

They handed the scroll over to the police, and the perpetrator was finally brought to justice for his crime. The ghost disappeared, and the castle was finally free of haunting and terror.

The children returned home with a sense of relief and a new adventure in their hearts.

THE SPOOKY ENCOUNTER with a ghost pirate

The wind whistled through the sails as the friends sailed across the sea on their little boat. They had decided to take a trip out on the sea for a little adventure. But little did they know that they were in for a spooky encounter.

Suddenly, they saw an old ship appear on the horizon. It looked like a pirate ship, with a skull on the bow and a black sail. They were intrigued and drove closer to take a closer look.

But as they got closer, they heard a strange music emanating from the ship. It sounded like a violin concert, but it was eerie and creepy. They went even closer and suddenly saw a man standing on the ship who looked like a ghost pirate.

He had a long black coat on and wore a tricorn hat on his head. His skin was pale and he had dark eyes. He looked at the friends and said in a deep, smoky voice, "You are brave, but you had better turn back. This is a cursed ship and anyone who enters it will be a part of it forever."

The friends were frightened, but also curious. They decided to defy the ghost pirate and board the ship. They climbed aboard and looked around. The ship was old and weathered, but it looked as if it had sailed recently.

Suddenly, they heard a strange noise from far away. It sounded like a howl and was getting closer. The ghost pirate laughed and said, "That's the curse on this ship. It will haunt us until we are all cursed."

The friends were horrified and tried to leave the ship, but it was too late. The curse had reached them and they all became ghost pirates. They now sail the cursed ship forever, hunting other adventurers who dare to enter their waters.

Since then, no one has ever seen the ship again, but some say that on a clear night they can hear the howl of the curse still wafting across the sea.

THE EERIE ENCOUNTER in the subway

Lena and Max were on their way to school and got on the subway as they do every morning. But when they got into the train car, they noticed that something was different than usual. The train was completely empty and there was an eerie silence.

The two children sat down and waited for the next station. But suddenly the train stopped and the doors did not open. Panic set in as they realized they were trapped in the subway.

At that moment, they heard an eerie laugh and a figure in a black hood stepped out of the shadows. It was a creepy ghost wandering around the subway.

Lena and Max tried to escape, but the ghost seemed to be chasing them and they couldn't escape it. Finally, they reached the end of the line and the ghost disappeared into the darkness.

From that day on, they told everyone about the eerie encounter in the subway, but no one believed them.

THE GHOSTLY ENCOUNTER in the abandoned hospital

Lena and Max had planned to explore the abandoned hospital. For a long time they had heard about this place, which was supposed to be haunted. It was an eerie place where no one spent time voluntarily.

The sun was slowly setting when Lena and Max entered the abandoned building. Everything was dusty and smelled musty. The walls were streaked with moisture and the paint was peeling.

As they moved deeper into the building, they suddenly heard a strange noise. It sounded like a whisper that seemed to come from everywhere. Lena and Max looked around, startled, but couldn't make out anything.

Suddenly, they heard a door slam. They followed the sound and found a door that moved on its own. It seemed to be opened by a ghostly hand.

Lena and Max could not believe their eyes when they saw the ghostly figure opening in front of them. It was a girl in a white dress, floating through the hallways. She seemed to come from another world.

Lena and Max followed the girl, who led them deeper into the abandoned hospital. She seemed to want to show them something. They finally came to a room where there was a hospital bed. On the bed lay a figure that did not move.

Lena and Max stepped closer and saw that it was a man. He seemed to be unconscious. The girl in the white dress was standing next to him and seemed to be watching over him.

Suddenly the door was pushed open and a group of men rushed into the room. They wore uniforms and carried weapons.

Lena and Max recognized them as police officers and told them about the man on the bed. The policemen examined the man and found that he had been kidnapped. They took him to a hospital and arrested the kidnappers.

Lena and Max were relieved that they could help and that the man was saved. The girl in the white dress suddenly disappeared and the ghostly apparitions stopped. Lena and Max knew they had a ghostly encounter they would never forget.

The cursed mask of the pharaoh

The three friends Emma, Max and Tom have always been fascinated by Egyptian mythology and culture. When they learned that there was an exhibition of artifacts from ancient Egypt in town, they were beside themselves.

The exhibition was housed in an old museum and when they got there, they noticed that something was strange. The atmosphere was gloomy and it seemed as if a hint of fear hung in the air. But curiosity prevailed and they went further into the exhibition.

But when they reached the pharaoh's mask, they suddenly felt an eerie presence. Emma thought that the eyes of the mask moved and were directed at them. Max and Tom thought they were imagining it.

But as they continued walking, they suddenly heard a noise. It sounded like a whisper. They followed the sound and came to a door that led to a secret room.

When they opened the door, they saw a figure in the corner that looked like the ghost of an Egyptian priest. He spoke to them and warned them not to touch Pharaoh's mask.

The three friends were frightened, but they knew they had to do something to save the mask and the museum. They asked the priest what they should do and he told them to take the mask back to its tomb to break the curse.

So they took the mask and set out for Pharaoh's tomb. The way was full of dangers, but they fought their way and finally reached the tomb.

They placed the mask on Pharaoh's sarcophagus and recited a prayer formula. Suddenly the tomb began to shake and a powerful energy discharged. The curse was broken.

The three friends returned to the museum and everything seemed normal. But they knew they had accomplished an important task and felt proud and brave.

THE UNCANNY ENCOUNTER with a curse

Lena and her friends were excited when they received an invitation to a party at an old mansion. They had heard that the house was cursed, but they wanted to dare anyway.

When they entered the house, they immediately felt an eerie atmosphere. The walls were covered with strange symbols, and dusty artifacts were lying around everywhere. Suddenly, they heard a noise and saw a shadowy figure walk by.

The children decided to explore the house. When they got to the basement, they found an old box with a dusty mask inside. Without thinking, Lena picked up the mask and put it on her face.

Suddenly she felt a sharp pain in her head and an eerie laugh sounded in her ear. The other children heard it too and ran out of the house in panic.

The next few days were a nightmare for Lena. She had terrible nightmares and felt an eerie presence around her. Finally, she went to see an expert who explained that she had put a curse on herself by putting on the cursed mask.

Lena and her friends decided to take the mask back to the mansion and return it to the place where it was found. When they put the mask back, they felt a sudden relief and knew that the curse was broken.

From that day on, Lena was more cautious about exploring abandoned houses and touching dusty artifacts. She had learned to be wary of creepy encounters and curses.

The mysterious haunting of the abandoned school

It was a stormy night and the clouds covered the moon. The group of friends, consisting of Max, Lisa, Tim and Sarah, decided to explore the abandoned school. They had heard about the rumors that the school was haunted and decided to get to the bottom of it.

When they entered the school, it immediately became dark and creepy. The walls were covered in graffiti and the doors creaked loudly. Suddenly, they heard a noise coming from one of the classrooms and decided to check it out.

When they entered the room, they saw a student in old clothes sitting at an old desk, crying quietly. The group asked if they could help her, but when the student turned around, she had a creepy smile on her face.

Suddenly they heard a voice saying, "You shouldn't be here. Leave this place before it's too late." The group was frightened and decided to leave, but the door was suddenly locked.

They heard footsteps and voices behind the door and thought they were being followed by ghosts or demons. The group decided to look for another way out and discovered a secret door behind a shelf.

They opened the door and found a staircase leading to the basement. As they went down the stairs, they heard screaming and eventually found a group of students involved in a ceremony to break a curse.

The group managed to save the students and break the curse. As they were leaving the school, they saw the student leaving the classroom and said goodbye to her. The group knew they would never go back to the school, but they were proud to have broken the curse and saved lives.

THE SPOOKY STORY OF the cursed village

Once upon a time there was a small village called Gomera. It was located deep in the forest and had a dark past. Many years ago, there had been a mysterious epidemic that took almost all the inhabitants. Those who survived were scarred for life and lived in constant fear of the curse that seemed to hover over the village.

When a few curious children decided to explore the cursed village, they had no idea what awaited them. They wandered through the forest and finally reached the abandoned village. Everything looked dilapidated, the houses were empty and the streets were deserted.

The children entered the first house they saw and found nothing but dust and dirt. But when they entered the second house, they suddenly heard a soft whisper. They looked around and noticed a ghostly figure floating through the room. The children were frightened and ran out of the house.

But there was no escape. Everywhere in the village they encountered ghosts and other eerie creatures. They were pursued by eerie voices and driven through the streets by invisible forces. Finally, the children managed to escape to an old church.

There they met an old man sitting in a corner who told them about the epidemic. He told them that the curse of the village had never been broken and that the spirits of the dead were still seeking revenge.

The children knew they had to act quickly to escape the cursed village. They decided to break the curse by finding an ancient scroll that supposedly held the key to solving the mystery.

They searched the village and finally found the scroll in an abandoned house. It was written in an ancient language and difficult to understand, but the children did not give up. They read the scroll aloud and suddenly the village was flooded with a bright light. The ghosts disappeared and the village was safe again.

The children returned home and told everyone about their scary experience in the cursed village. But they also knew that they had broken the curse and that Gomera was now a safe place to live again.

The mysterious disappearance of the detective

It was a sunny day in autumn and the leaves on the trees had already begun to turn red and yellow. Detectives Max and Mia were on their way to their next case when suddenly their colleague and friend, the famous detective Thomas, disappeared. He had given them a secret assignment that they now had to solve on their own.

The two detectives were worried and set out to find clues. They searched his office and found a coded message. After a few hours, they deciphered it and realized that it was an address. They immediately headed there and found an old abandoned building.

When they opened the door, they heard strange noises and felt an eerie presence. They searched the building and finally found a hidden door that led to an underground room. There they found a strange machine they didn't recognize and another encrypted message.

Again, they decoded the message and found that Thomas had been kidnapped by a secret crime syndicate for getting too close to the truth. The message also contained clues to a place where Thomas was being held captive.

The detectives headed there and found Thomas in an old abandoned building, bound and gagged. They freed him and took him to safety. Thomas thanked them and gave them the next clue to their next case.

Detectives Max and Mia had rescued their friend and solved the case. They were relieved and proud of themselves. But they also knew that there would be many more adventures and cases to look forward to.

THE GHOSTLY ENCOUNTER in the castle museum

Emma and Tom were excited when they entered the castle museum. The old paintings, historical objects and richly decorated furniture fascinated the two friends. But when they found themselves in a room with antique mirrors, things suddenly got creepy.

One mirror seemed different from the others. It was like a gateway to another world. Emma and Tom dared to look inside and suddenly they saw themselves in another dimension.

Everything was dark and eerie. They heard footsteps and voices, but couldn't see anyone. As they walked through the dark corridors of the castle, they encountered a ghostly knight. He seemed to come from another time and warned the two friends that they should leave the castle before it was too late.

But Emma and Tom did not want to give up. They thought they had a job to do to return from the other dimension. They followed the ghostly knight through the castle until they came across a scroll hidden in an old desk.

The knight explained that the scroll held the key to returning to their own world, but that it was guarded by an evil spirit. Emma and Tom dared to fight the ghost, and after a hard battle, they were able to free the scroll.

When they were back in their own world, Emma and Tom were relieved and excited at the same time. They had a ghostly encounter at the castle museum, but they had also completed an important task and found a treasure that they would treasure in the future.

The spooky encounter with a shadowy creature

Anna and Tim were walking in an old abandoned house when suddenly an eerie feeling came over them. It was as if they were being watched. They turned around, but no one was there.

"What's going on?" asked Tim.

"I don't know," said Anna. "It feels like someone is following us."

Suddenly, a shadow appeared on the wall, moving as if it had a life of its own. The two children looked at each other and knew they were not alone.

Then they heard a strange whisper that grew louder and louder until it finally became an eerie laugh. They turned around and saw a shadow creature standing in front of them.

The shadow creature was tall and gloomy and seemed to come from another world. It had no facial features, but its eyes glowed red.

Anna and Tim wanted to escape, but the shadow creature blocked their way. It seemed scary and dangerous.

Suddenly Anna remembered something she had read in a book. "We have to drive the shadow creature away with light," she whispered to Tim.

They searched in their bag and found a flashlight. When they turned on the light, the shadow creature flinched and disappeared.

Anna and Tim were relieved, but also very excited. They had never seen a shadow creature before, and they wondered what it was and where it came from.

They decided to investigate the shadow creature and started searching the Internet for information. Eventually they found out that it was a creature from another world that could only be driven away with light.

From that day on, Anna and Tim were even more curious about the supernatural and began to search for more mysteries and adventures.

THE CURSED DOLL IN the antique shop

The sun blazed down on Tim's head as he stopped in front of an old antique store. The store had a weathered sign that read "Antiques O'Connell" in gold letters. Tim knew he should be on his way to soccer practice, but he just couldn't resist. He was curious about the store that always looked so mysterious.

When Tim opened the door, he expected a bell to ring. Instead, it was silent. A dull smell filled his nose as he looked around. The antique store was full of shelves and display cases showing old books, paintings, and figurines. Tim sensed he was being watched and turned around. But there was no one there.

Then Tim noticed a display case covered by a red velvet curtain. He stepped closer and pulled the curtain aside. In the glass case was an old doll with long black hair and a pale face. The doll wore an old, tattered dress that looked like it was from a horror movie.

Suddenly, Tim heard a soft laugh behind him. He turned around, but no one was there. The laughter grew louder and finally Tim saw a figure emerge from the shadows. It was an old woman with a creepy grin on her face.

"The doll is cursed," the woman said in a raspy voice. "She brings bad luck and death. If you buy her, you will regret it."

Tim couldn't take his eyes off the woman's doll. He felt like he was hypnotized. He had to have this doll.

The woman smiled wider and handed him the doll. "Maybe we'll see each other again soon," she said, then disappeared into the shadows.

Tim ran out of the store as if the devil were chasing him. He didn't know what he had done. He felt like he had just experienced something scary and terrible.

The next day, Tim didn't show up for practice. His friends got worried and decided to go to his house. When they arrived, they found Tim's room empty. The doll he had bought yesterday was lying on the bed. Since then, Tim was never seen again.

The mysterious haunting of the old mill

Max and his friends were wandering through the forest, looking for a hidden waterfall. Suddenly they discovered an old, dilapidated mill. Max had heard a lot about the mill and was eager to go inside. But his friends were skeptical, because they said it was haunted.

Max didn't give up and persuaded his friends to go inside the old mill with him. Once inside, they heard strange noises and felt an eerie presence. Suddenly, the millstones started turning even though no one was operating them. One of the friends stumbled and fell to the floor. As he did so, he discovered a secret door.

They opened the door and found an old room full of treasures. But when Max opened a treasure chest, the ghosts of the former miller's family awoke and chased the children out of the mill.

On the way home, everyone was very excited about what they had experienced. Max, however, was very sad because he had not been able to save the treasure. But his friends told him that the adventure was worth much more than any treasure. Max agreed and vowed to explore more scary places.

THE SPOOKY STORY OF the cursed cemetery

It was a dark and stormy night. The children Emma, Tim and Lukas were on their way home from the cinema when they decided to take a shortcut through the cemetery. They thought it was a good idea to save time, but it was a mistake.

When they entered the cemetery, they noticed that all the graves were open and the graves were empty. All of a sudden, they heard a strange noise and saw a figure coming towards them. It was a man with a black cloak and a hood, holding a lighted candle in his hand.

The children were frightened and ran for their lives. They did not look back until they finally reached the exit. They thought they were safe, but suddenly they heard footsteps behind them. They turned around and saw the man chasing them.

They ran as fast as they could and finally they reached the exit. But when they turned around, they saw the man in the hood with the lit candle standing at the entrance gate. They were sure that he was a ghost.

Since that day, the cemetery was off limits for the children. They told their friends about their creepy encounter and no one ever wanted to go there again. It was said that the cemetery was cursed and that anyone who entered it would be haunted by a ghost.

The children didn't believe it, but they were sure they would never set foot in the cemetery again. The memories of their creepy encounter will haunt them for a long time.

The mysterious disappearance of the farmer

In a small village once lived a farmer named Peter. One day he disappeared without a trace and no one knew what had happened. His family and friends searched everywhere for him, but they found no trace. The police couldn't help either because there was no evidence of a crime.

But then the villagers heard rumors about a mysterious figure wandering around the cemetery at night. Some said it was the ghost of Peter, who was seeking revenge for being treated unjustly. Others believed it was a demon or an evil spirit haunting the village.

A few brave children decided to get to the bottom of it. They waited until dark and went to the cemetery. There they actually saw a figure that seemed to shimmer in the moonlight. They followed it carefully and finally came to an abandoned barn on the outskirts of the village.

As they approached, they heard strange noises and voices. The children hardly dared to come closer, but their curiosity drove them on. They crept around the building and discovered a secret hiding place filled with items they had never seen before.

But before they could take a closer look, they were spotted by the mysterious figure. They tried to run away, but they were pursued by the creature. Finally, they managed to escape and return to the village.

They told their friends and adults about the secret hiding place and the mysterious figure. The police investigated the barn and found evidence that Peter had been held captive there. The perpetrators were eventually arrested and Peter was rescued.

The village was relieved that the case had been solved, but the children remembered the spooky encounter with the ghost and the secret hiding place for a long time.

THE GHOSTLY ENCOUNTER in the abandoned mine

Siblings Max and Lisa were always looking for new adventures. One day they heard about an old abandoned mine that was supposedly cursed. No one had dared to enter it since a terrible accident had happened, killing several workers.

Max and Lisa, however, were determined to unravel the mystery of the mine and decided to set out. They found the mine after some time and although they were standing in front of it, they suddenly had the feeling that something was wrong. An icy wind was blowing through the area and it seemed as if the mine was surrounded by an invisible force field.

They slowly ventured inside and were surrounded by darkness. Lisa held the flashlight while Max was armed with a hammer and chisel to clear any possible obstacles. Suddenly they heard a noise and it got louder and louder, as if something was approaching.

Max and Lisa got scared and wanted to turn back immediately, but suddenly they saw a white being standing right in front of them. It looked like a ghost, with glowing eyes and a pale body.

They froze and did not dare to move. The being floated directly toward them and seemed to read their minds. It whispered in a ghostly voice, "You are not afraid to die? Then come with me."

Max and Lisa were transfixed as they followed the spirit and it led them to an old, rusty elevator. Without hesitation, they got in and descended deep inside the mine.

When they reached the bottom, they saw a glowing crystal cave filled with treasures. The spirit told them they could take anything they wanted, but they had to pay a price - they had to free him and his soul from the mine.

Max and Lisa were willing to do anything to escape from the mine, so they agreed to the deal. They worked hard and successfully to free the ghost and his soul, and when they left the mine, they were proud of what they had accomplished.

They had solved the mystery of the cursed mine and gained a valuable treasure in the process, but most importantly, they had helped a spirit find peace.

The eerie encounter with a spectre

It was a stormy night and Mia couldn't sleep. The wind howled around the house and raindrops pattered against the window. Suddenly she heard a strange sound coming from her closet. It was a strange whisper that sent a shiver down her spine.

Mia decided to confront the noise. She stood up and opened the closet. The moment she opened the door, she was hit by an icy gust of wind that blotted out the light in the room. Mia heard a deep growling sound and sensed that something sinister was in the room.

Suddenly, a spectre appeared - a ghostly creature with glowing eyes and long, pointed claws. It seemed to come out of the closet and slowly floated toward Mia. She couldn't move or scream, she was paralyzed.

But then she remembered an old saying: ghosts are afraid of light. Mia reached for her flashlight and turned it on. The bugbear screamed out and disappeared in a swirl of darkness.

Mia breathed a sigh of relief and looked around the room. All was quiet and the eerie sound had disappeared. She decided to lie down again and tried to fall asleep. But this time she was no longer afraid, because she knew that she had defeated the spectre.

The cursed library of dark magic

The three friends Max, Emma and Tom were looking for a new adventure. One day they heard about a library that was supposed to be full of forbidden and dangerous books about dark magic. No one knew who ran the library or where it was located, but that didn't stop the friends from searching for it.

They searched libraries and archives, asked librarians and booksellers, but no one seemed to have ever heard of such a library. Finally, they received a tip from a mysterious stranger in a bookstore. He whispered to them that the library was hidden somewhere near the old cemetery.

The friends immediately made their way to the cemetery and eventually discovered a door leading into the ground. They opened the door and descended a flight of stairs into a dark, musty room. Here, indeed, was the library of dark magic.

The shelves were full of old and dusty books, bound in leather and decorated with golden letters. The friends searched the shelves and found books about black magic, curses and spells they had never seen before. Suddenly they heard a voice warning them to leave the library and never come back.

But the friends were too curious and started reading the books and doing experiments with magic. But this had dire consequences. The books were cursed and the friends had accidentally triggered a curse. The books came to life and attacked the friends. A horde of shadow creatures crawled out of the pages of the books and began chasing the friends.

The friends ran for their lives and fought the shadow creatures. But the curse seemed invincible. Finally, they managed to find the exit and escape from the library. Once outside, they looked around and realized that the graveyard and the library were gone.

The friends were relieved that they had escaped, but they knew that the curse would haunt them for a long time. They vowed never to return to the dark magic library and to stay away from that kind of magic.

The mysterious haunting of the old mansion by the lake

The sun was already low in the sky when the four friends finally arrived in front of the old mansion by the lake. It was an impressive mansion that must have once been magnificent and proud. But now it was just an abandoned and gloomy ruin.

"Looks like no one has lived here for years," Leo noted, his gaze sliding over the broken windows and weathered plaster.

"It looks like a haunted house," Marie whispered, shuddering at the thought that they were about to go inside.

"Stop chatting and come with me," Tim urged, entering the house first.

Inside, it was even darker and creepier than outside. The air smelled damp and musty and it seemed as if every step on the rotten wooden floor made the entire house shake.

"What the hell is that?" shouted Lina suddenly, pointing to something at the end of the hall.

The friends followed her pointing and stared at a shadowy outline slowly moving toward them.

"A ghost," Marie screamed and tried to flee, but Tim held her tight.

"It's not a ghost, it's just an optical illusion," he reassured her and boldly walked toward the outline.

As he got closer, he realized it was just a large mirror that looked like a shadow in the dim light of the hallway.

Relieved, the friends breathed a sigh of relief, but when they looked at the mirror, they saw that it was not just any mirror, but an antique mirror decorated with carvings.

"Let's get out of here," Marie demanded, and the friends hurried out of the house.

Only when they were outside did they dare look back. They saw the mirror sparkling in the window of the house, whispering an eerie message to them.

"You will come back," he whispered, and an icy chill ran down the friends' spines.

They ran away, vowing never to return.

THE SPOOKY STORY OF the cursed circus

The sun had already set when the children discovered the abandoned circus. They were curious and eager to see the place. As they got closer, they felt an eerie coldness surround them. Rusty bars, weathered tents and broken props were everywhere. The children walked through the entrance and entered a world of darkness and shadows.

Suddenly, they heard sounds from a distance that sounded like clowns laughing. But they knew it was impossible, because the circus was deserted. But when they turned around, they saw a group of clowns approaching them. They wore sad and sinister faces, and their eyes were blank and dead.

The children ran, but the clowns followed them. They ran through the circus and everywhere they went they saw creepy things: a tent full of bloody knives, a maze of mirrors that showed distorted reflections, and a ring full of animals that were trapped and caged.

When they finally reached a dark corner, the clowns stopped and disappeared. The children were exhausted and frightened when they realized they were at a dead end. Then they heard a voice coming from a rusted speaker, "Welcome to the Circus of the Cursed. Your time here is up."

The children were terrified and knew they had to flee quickly. They ran for their lives until they finally reached the exit. Once outside, they looked back and noticed that the circus was gone, as if it had never been there.

The children were relieved that they had escaped, but they knew they would never return. The Circus of the Cursed would remain in their memories forever.

The mysterious disappearance of the ship's crew

The sun blazed hotly on the deck of the cruise ship as passengers happily sipped their cocktails and relaxed on their deck chairs. But suddenly the idyll was interrupted when the ship made an unexpected course change and set course for a deserted island.

Young detective Max and his friends were among the passengers, and they were concerned about the sudden change of course. They suspected that something was wrong and decided to investigate on their own.

When they reached the island, they found the abandoned ship of the crew, but there was no trace of the people. The group began searching the island and eventually came across an old hut on the beach. Inside the hut, they found evidence that something terrible had happened and decided to keep searching.

As they wandered through the jungle, they were accompanied by an eerie sound that seemed to come from everywhere. Suddenly, one of them was grabbed by an invisible force and disappeared into the darkness.

The remaining friends ran for their lives and eventually ended up in a cave, where they found the missing person and the rest of the ship's crew. But they were not alone - a dark figure with glowing eyes appeared and pursued them through the cave.

It was an escape filled with adrenaline as they ran for their lives trying to get out of the cave. Finally, they reached the shore where a small boat was waiting for them and escaped just in time.

When they reached the mainland, they were relieved to have escaped, but also worried about the fate of the ship's crew and the dark figure that had been chasing them. Max and his friends vowed to solve the case and find out the truth, no matter how creepy or scary it might be.

THE GHOSTLY ENCOUNTER in the old theater

The four friends had had a great day at the amusement park. But the evening had already fallen and they decided to watch one more show at the old theater. The theater had been around for many years and many say it was haunted.

The friends bought their tickets and found their seats. The theater was only half full, but the atmosphere was still spooky. During the performance, they could hear strange noises that seemed to come from the walls. When the performance was over, the four remained seated to take a closer look at the theater.

But suddenly they heard a strange noise. It sounded like the clatter of heels on the floor. They turned around and saw a ghostly figure standing on the stage. It was a girl in an old theater costume. She seemed to be looking right through them.

The friends were fascinated and scared at the same time. They walked closer to the stage to get a closer look at the figure. But as they climbed the steps, the figure seemed to move farther and farther away from them.

Suddenly, they felt an icy breeze brush across their backs. They turned around and saw that the girl was now standing right behind them. She seemed to want to say something to them, but her words could not be heard.

The friends were so fascinated by the ghost that they forgot they were in a haunted theater. Suddenly it went dark and they heard the clatter of heels coming towards them. They ran for their lives and just barely managed to escape from the theater.

They knew they would never enter that creepy place again. But still, it was an exciting and unforgettable adventure that they would never forget.

Impressum

LIOM LIOM
AUF DER HÖH 13A
35447 REISKIRCHEN
KONTAKT
E-MAIL: sl350sl@gmx.de

Don't miss out!

Visit the website below and you can sign up to receive emails whenever Liom Liom publishes a new book. There's no charge and no obligation.

https://books2read.com/r/B-A-AOUW-OGQGC

Did you love *Scary Stories for Children*? Then you should read *Adventure in Dino Land*[1] by Liom Liom!

Experience exciting adventures in Dino Land together with Pino and his friends! This paperback brings together all the stories in a fantastic collection that will delight children between the ages of 6 and 8. Join Pino and his friends as they discover a mysterious crystal, return to Dino Land, care for a new baby dinosaur, and many more exciting events. But not only exciting adventures await the little readers. Each story also holds a valuable moral that is conveyed in a child-frindly way. Whether it's about friendship, responsibility or cohesion - Pino and his friends

---

1. https://books2read.com/u/ml8PMB

2. https://books2read.com/u/ml8PMB

always stand up for each other and show how important it is to be there for each other. The handy paperback book is perfect for little hands and is ideal for reading aloud or reading by yourself. The child-friendly language and loving stories take young readers on an exciting journey to Dino Land.